A New Heart for Christmas

Debbie G. Harman

Covenant Communications, Inc.

Covenant

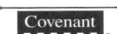

This story is dedicated to D Bob and Matthew
and to all others who have special needs.
Thank you for teaching us the meaning of
unconditional love.

I would like to acknowledge Stacey Owen
and all others at Covenant Communications
who worked on this story.
Thank you for making it a success.

Red Gloves Hold Heart Shaped Snowball © mrPliskin , iStockphoto.com

Cover design copyright © 2013 by Covenant Communications, Inc.

Published by Covenant Communications, Inc.
American Fork, Utah

Printed in the United States of America
First Printing: October 2013

19 18 17 16 15 14 13   10 9 8 7 6 5 4 3 2 1

ISBN 978-1-62108-585-0

-1-

IT WAS LATE NOVEMBER. WINTER was just settling into the small valley where we had built our home. I gazed out the kitchen window, elbow deep in hot, sudsy dishwater.

It's been fifteen years, I thought as I watched large flakes of snow whip through the air. A few inches had already piled onto the sturdy ponderosa just a few feet from my position. Hard to believe the massive evergreen was once a scraggy twig my husband planted just days after we moved in.

That was the year Matthew was born. This had been a great place to raise our two boys. But the years had passed so fast, our boys now in their teens. I wished I could freeze them in time, keep them with me a little longer.

Just then Bobby, my oldest son, came through the front door singing, "It's beginning to look a lot like Christmas," and dragging a trail of snow all the way to the kitchen. "We must have gotten six or seven inches," he squealed, "and it's still coming down."

"Look at your shoes!" I cried, tossing him a towel. He continued belting out the lyrics to the carol with his typical humor as he wiped the wet snow from the hardwood floor and danced his way back to my side.

"Sorry 'bout the snow, Mom," he said, leaning over and giving my shoulder a squeeze. He dropped the wet towel on the table and began unpacking a pile of clothes from his gym bag.

"Oh yeah, Mom, can you wash my uniform today?" he asked. "Bus leaves early tomorrow." He tipped his head and gave me his big wide smile. I nodded and continued clearing the breakfast dishes. This time of year, it seemed like washing his uniform was a daily task.

"Is Matthew still sleeping? I gotta thank him for coming to my game last night."

"He was when I last checked," I answered, "but you can wake him."

He ran out the front door and came right back with a handful of snow he was forming into a ball.

"I gotta show him!" Bobby said with excitement, and down the hall he went. I couldn't hear what they were saying, but their voices flowed like a melody from Matthew's bedroom into the kitchen.

The boys had been close as children, but as Bobby had gotten older, he was often annoyed with Matthew. It had only been a couple months since Bobby started spending time with his brother again. Maybe it was that Bobby was a senior and knew he'd be leaving home soon, or maybe it was Matthew's condition that got to Bobby. I wasn't sure what caused the change, but I was grateful to have them bonding as brothers again.

After some time Bobby was back in the kitchen again. "Love you, Mom," he said, giving me a firm hug and kissing my cheek.

"I love you too." I stood silent, taking in the moment. I couldn't quite put my finger on it—the change in him—but my son was different somehow.

He'd always been a good boy. Bobby had never given us any trouble. He was respectful and obedient, and he earned top grades. But recently he seemed different. Something about him radiated. He stayed home more and spent more time with our family. He was happier than I had ever seen him.

As soon as the door closed, it opened again. Bobby popped his head back in and exclaimed, "This snow is awesome!"

I laughed and walked to the living room window just in time to watch him spinning away, sliding a bit in the new fallen snow.

That's quite a storm blowing out there, I thought as I went to check on Matthew.

Our son Matthew, now fifteen, was born with Down syndrome, a chromosomal disorder. Along with the many other physical and mental challenges he faced, Matthew also had a heart condition. Even after the many surgeries and the therapy Matthew had endured, his doctor informed us that our son's fragile heart likely wouldn't make it another year. "His only hope," we were told, "is a heart transplant."

That was July, and in the months that followed, as we watched the weather change and the leaves fall from the trees, we were troubled to see Matthew's strength fall as well. He continued to get weaker and weaker until, finally, he was confined to a wheelchair. But unlike the leaves—that fell, dried up, and blew away—Matthew's spirit refused to die, and his optimism soared ever higher. Each morning as I entered the kitchen, he was always there to greet me.

"Hi, Mom. Wha for breakfuss?" he'd ask, already dressed, his face washed and hair combed. He was always the first one ready, and he did it without anybody's help.

"I can do mysef," he told us constantly, and he did. Matthew had done everything for himself. He'd fed himself, bathed himself, pulled himself into and out of his chair, and even wheeled himself wherever he wanted to go.

But after Thanksgiving, his condition had worsened. Matthew wasn't there to greet me in the mornings. He was too weak to get out of bed. He had lost his appetite—an odd thing for Matthew because he was always hungry. That's when I really began to pray for a miracle.

Matthew's bedroom door was open, and I peeked in; he had rolled over on his side, asleep again. His hair, badly matted in back, let me know it had been a hard night. Matthew's heart condition caused stress on his lungs. Although he had oxygen, sometimes he pulled the tubes out in his sleep. I checked the tubes; they were in. *Bobby must have fixed them,* I concluded. I tucked the soft flannel blanket around Matthew's shoulders.

Just then, I caught a glimpse of a crisp white paper next to the headboard. The still-evident creases made it obvious that it had been folded, but now it lay open just inches from the edge of the bed, ready to slip onto the floor. Without even trying, I managed to read the handwriting across the top.

To my best brother, Matthew,

It's a letter, I realized and averted my eyes out of respect for the boys' privacy. I quietly picked up the paper and slowly began to fold it, hoping to not wake Matthew. But as luck would have it, he rolled over and mumbled, "Thas my ledder fom Bobby. He gave to me."

"Oh, that was nice," I answered. "I'll put it right here in your drawer, okay?"

"You read it genn?" he asked.

"Sure." I unfolded the paper and read aloud.

Matthew interrupted often, asking me, "Read that part genn?"

So I would repeat the line. I read the last part of the letter so many times I had it memorized.

So that's the Christmas miracle I'm praying for. I don't want any presents this year. All I want for Christmas is to change my heart into a heart like yours.

I brushed away a few tears, folded the letter, and placed it among the others in the top drawer of his dresser. This wasn't the first letter Bobby had given to Matthew. There were plenty.

When Matthew was learning to read, his teacher suggested that we find something that Matthew loved and then try to get him to read about it. One evening shortly thereafter, Bobby came into the family room and gave Matthew a folded piece of paper.

"It's a letter," Bobby said with a little pride. "I wrote it to you."

Matthew quickly unfolded it, but he struggled with the words. I had to read most of it. Then he folded and unfolded that letter at least twenty times, each time asking his dad or me to help him read it. We were amazed that Bobby could have known this would help, but it did, and from that day, Bobby wrote Matthew lots of letters. And Matthew kept every one inside the top drawer of his dresser.

But as the boys grew and Bobby's life became more involved, he stopped writing letters. This was the first one I knew of in a long time.

"Bobby say he wants heart like mine. He say I have bess heart," Matthew whispered.

He was so exhausted! "Well, Bobby's right about that. You do have the best heart."

"I pray for Bobby have heart like mine."

"That's a good idea." I smiled. "But you better sleep first, okay?"

"Okay," he conceded and closed his eyes.

For Matthew, prayer had never been optional. He prayed for everything. And he made sure we prayed for everything too. We prayed every morning and night. He wouldn't let us eat a meal until we said a prayer. Bobby couldn't play in a game and we couldn't get in the car until we'd prayed. And even when he had almost no strength at all, Matthew managed to pull himself to a sitting position so he could bow his head when he prayed.

I softly stroked the side of his face. He looked so frail; I couldn't help but question how many days we had left with him.

The phone rang, startling me a bit. I quietly left Matthew's room and hurried into the kitchen. My heart raced as I glanced at the clock on the stove—8:27. Have they found a heart for Matthew? My hopes were high as I reached for the phone.

"Mrs. Bailey?" came a man's voice.

"Yes," I answered.

"Your son Bobby has been in an accident." The room started spinning.

What had he said? Bobby was just here. How could it be? *Who is this?* I wanted to ask. *Where's Bobby?* So many questions, but I couldn't open my mouth. I just stood there. The voice continued. "He's been taken by helicopter to the university hospital."

So many frightening images flashed through my mind, but the word *hospital* brought instant hope. A feeling of peace surrounded me. The hospital had always been a place of safety for my family. We'd witnessed one miracle after another there.

Not just for Matthew, but also for the many of children we had met over the years.

Everything will be okay, I thought.

The minute I hung up, my husband called. He too had just been informed about Bobby.

"I'm coming to get you," he said. "Call Kathy to see if she can stay with Matthew."

Matthew! I rushed back to check on him.

When I pushed open his bedroom door, I was surprised to see he wasn't in bed. Instead, I saw him kneeling—well, on his knees, but mostly he was resting against the bed. He didn't have enough strength to kneel. I backed into the hallway and waited. Although it wasn't unusual to see Matthew pray, it had been quite a while since I had seen him kneeling.

"Amen," he said out loud and then tried to pull himself up.

"Do you need help?" I asked, rushing to his side. He fell into my arms, even weaker than before. As I strained to lift him onto the bed, my heart was torn. How could I leave him? But I had to go to Bobby. Then, it was as if he knew my very thoughts.

"We're goin have miraco," he said, looking up into my face.

"A miracle?" I asked.

"Yes, a miraco."

I kissed him on the head. "Well, if anyone can get us a miracle, I think it's you."

"Yeah, tha wha Bobby said!" He smiled, his eyes closed; he was too tired to hold them open.

"Is it okay if Aunt Kathy comes to take care of you?" I asked.

"I like Kathy. She nice." His voice was faint. It must have taken everything he had to get out of bed. I pulled the covers back over him and checked his oxygen. I bent down and kissed him again.

"I love you," I whispered, but he was already asleep.

There were so many people who helped me with Matthew. It would have been easy to call anyone. But my sister lived just minutes away, and she could stay with Matthew overnight if needed. She was there in no time, offering much needed words of comfort.

The hospital was about an hour's drive, but it seemed much longer. My husband was silent. I couldn't talk either, but my thoughts continued racing.

Bobby was only two when Matthew came along. I'd always felt a little guilty that Bobby was somewhat neglected with all the attention his brother needed. But it never seemed to bother him. Bobby thrived in every way. But now, at seventeen, in his last year of high school, so much of our attention had suddenly shifted to him. My thoughts, my prayers, and my energy were focused on Bobby.

Basketball season had just begun. Bobby was a star player. As the point guard, he had led his team to many victories, even a state championship his junior year. "A real coach's dream," Coach Hughes often told me. They were undefeated so far in the region and hoping for another state title. Bobby already had scholarship offers; his future looked so promising.

"I wonder if he'll be able to play ball," I thought out loud.

My husband, Robert, mumbled some response. He was obviously as deep in thought as I had been.

"What are you thinking about?" I asked.

"Last night," he answered.

"The game?" I pressed.

"No, before the game. When we were in Matthew's room, after family prayer. I was thinking about what Bobby told Matthew." Robert continued, but I was barely listening. My mind was already going over the events of the previous night.

After Matthew had prayed, Bobby leaned over to him, thanked him for his prayer, and said, "Don't be scared. I know God listens to your prayers." Then Bobby had gotten emotional. He'd quickly swept the back of his hand across both eyes in an attempt to hide his tears. "Matthew, tonight I'm dedicating my game to you," he continued, choking back the tears. "Every basket I make is gonna be for you!"

It was hard, but Matthew was determined to be at the game. And Bobby kept his word. Every time he made a basket, he turned and pointed to Matthew. Matthew got so excited. And so did the crowd. It didn't take long for the fans to notice Bobby pointing to Matthew. After a while, whenever Bobby made a basket, the students started chanting "Matthew, Matthew." A warm spirit swept through the entire gymnasium.

It really had been Bobby's best game. He'd had nine steals and scored an amazing thirty-three points. Suddenly, I felt a sharp tightening in my chest. Did my husband know something I didn't?

"What is it?" I asked. "What do you know?"

He turned and looked straight into my eyes. His were swollen and red; he was crying. "I feel like," he stammered between sobbing tears. "I feel like Bobby's gone."

That's it? Just like that? I'd been sitting there wondering if there was any possibility that Bobby would play basketball again, and his father was already grieving for him? I didn't know whether to be mad at him or to trust his feeling. Neither was good, so I kept clinging to the hope that everything would be okay. It had to be okay! *Bobby was just driving to school. The speed limit is only thirty-five. How bad could it be?*

When we finally arrived at the hospital, Derrick Miller's parents met us in the waiting room. *Of course*, I realized. *Derrick must have been with Bobby.*

Derrick was Bobby's best friend. He was a blue-eyed towhead just like Bobby. When they were kids, everyone thought they were brothers. They played Little League together and, as chance would have it, on the same team every year. Now in high school, it was fun to watch them play basketball together. The two were inseparable. So I wasn't surprised to see Derrick's parents here.

His mother's face was pale. Her hands trembled as she reached toward me. "We are so sorry."

Sorry? What were they sorry for?

"We've seen Derrick," his father said, "but they won't let us see Bobby."

"Why?" I asked. "Is it really that bad?" They both gazed at the ground.

"I don't understand," his father said, slowly looking up at me. "Derrick said Bobby asked him to drive."

My mind started spinning. Why would Bobby ask Derrick to drive? His car was his baby. He never let anyone drive it.

"Derrick was turning left on Highway 89," Mr. Miller continued. "He said he didn't see the truck."

A truck? The image immediately formed in my head: a truck slamming into my son's car. I remembered Bobby driving away. The snow was heavy and slick.

The horrid thoughts were interrupted as I noticed an older man walking toward us. He was tall and thin, very thin. Even in the heavy coat draped over him, it was evident he didn't eat well. His hair, gray and scraggly, came down over his ears. His face was pale, his eyes sunken and hollow. He stopped about a foot away, lowering his head. His long fingers nervously slid back and forth around the rim of a badly worn cap. His voice was trembling, "You must be the young man's parents. I'm real sorry, folks. I tried to stop, but the road—it was so slick." Even with his head down, I could see the tears pooling in his eyes.

The stranger was obviously the truck driver. Robert reached forward and placed his hand on the man's shoulder.

"Thank you. Are you okay?" my husband asked, squeezing gently in an effort to comfort the man.

"Mr. and Mrs. Bailey?" came a woman's voice from the corner of the room. A young nurse dressed in light purple scrubs—and probably still in college—stood in the hallway. We followed her into the cold, dimly lit intensive care unit. I wasn't prepared.

Of all the surgeries we had been through with Matthew, none of them frightened me as this sight did on this day. I knew the minute I saw Bobby that something was missing. That wasn't our boy. Instinctively, I knew Robert was right. I collapsed into his arms and began to sob. He joined in, and together we held each other and cried.

Sometime later, the doctor entered. I think he asked questions. Maybe we answered; I don't remember. Most of the conversation is still a blur. I took Bobby's lifeless hand in mine, pleading endlessly with God to spare him. Meanwhile, pieces, small fragments of the doctor's conversation found their way into my head. Things like, "Severe trauma to his brain," and "He'll be a vegetable." Each comment tearing away a piece of my hope until one sentence penetrated straight to my heart, like a knife, twisting and cutting every fiber: "Even if Bobby survives, he'll have to be on the machine. He can't live without it." The diagnosis was sharp. I couldn't ignore the reality.

Bobby's life is in our hands . . . but I can't pull the plug on my son. I can't!

As I tried to adjust to the idea of it, the doctor continued. "If you want to donate his organs, you don't have much time."

His organs? My son is still alive and they're already making plans for his organs? The vultures! I gently rubbed my thumb over Bobby's fingers. "Please come back. Don't leave us," I begged.

Long after the doctor had left the room, Robert's voice finally broke the silence. "What do you think?" He stood on the opposite side of the bed holding Bobby's other hand.

"I can't think about anything," I answered.

"I know what you're feeling," he assured me. "This is hard for me too." He reached up and placed his hand on the side of Bobby's face. "But we have to think about what's best for everyone. Bobby's gone. You know that. I know you know it. We have to accept it." His voice was cracking. I knew he was holding back. He swallowed hard and looked over at me. "Bobby's gone. But we have a chance to save Matthew. This may be the answer to our prayers."

"Our prayers?" I ask, angry and bewildered. "How can this be the answer to our prayers?"

"Well, how did you think it worked?" His voice was gentle.

"What do you mean?"

"Every time we prayed that Matthew would get a new heart, where did you think that heart would come from?"

"I guess I never really thought about it. Did you?"

"Yes," he admitted. "I've thought about it a lot." He reached across the bed and placed his hand over mine. "And to be honest, I've felt a little selfish pleading with God for Matthew because I knew that it meant someone, somewhere, would be suffering just as we are now."

I honestly hadn't thought about it that way before. It seemed so cruel.

"Do you wish it was Derrick?" he asked.

"What? Of course not!" How could he ask such a thing?

"If Bobby had been driving, Derrick would be the one in this bed," he said. I tried to comprehend it.

"Could you ask Derrick's parents to donate his heart to Matthew?" he questioned, looking at me with all sincerity. I didn't answer.

"Well, I couldn't, and I think God knows I couldn't." He dropped his head and gripped Bobby's hand in his. For some reason the last line of Bobby's letter surfaced in my head.

✱ *So that's the Christmas miracle I'm praying for. I don't want any presents this year. All I want for Christmas is to change my heart into a heart like yours.*

It was too much for me to take in. Just a few hours ago, Bobby had been dancing around the house singing Christmas carols and asking me to wash his uniform.

My husband's voice interrupted my thoughts. "So here's our choice," he said, now pushing the tears away constantly and choking on every word. "Bobby on a machine with no life at all or Matthew with a chance. Finally, a chance for a life that he has never been able to have."

-2-

THE DAYS THAT FOLLOWED THE surgery were long and lonely. Even with the many friends and family visiting, I could not escape my grief. I was grateful for their concern and help. I was. I don't think I could have made it without them. It seemed that each time I felt I couldn't go on, I received a card in the mail or a phone call or someone showed up at the door. That's what got me through the days. But when the nights came, when the house was still and quiet and I couldn't sleep, that's when the loss seemed more than I could endure.

But I did endure. With the help of God and my husband, I did endure. The days slowly turned into weeks, and finally, Matthew came home.

It helped to have Matthew back. I needed someone to look after, and it was nice to have his optimistic spirit around again. Time seemed to pass more quickly. I was feeling better every day.

But then Christmas Eve came.

Someone had told me, "As time passes, you don't feel the pain as often, but when it comes, it hurts just as much." And that's how Christmas Eve was.

Derrick came to visit us early one day. When I opened the door and saw him standing on the porch, instinctively I turned to call for Bobby.

But Bobby was gone. The pain, all of it, instantly hit me again. I couldn't speak.

"Hi, Derrick. Come on in." I heard my husband's voice behind me.

Derrick hesitated. It was obvious this was hard for him. My heart softened a little. I hadn't considered before now how much he must be hurting. With a little coaxing, we got him into the living room, where he sat nervously at the edge of an armchair. Finally, he began to speak.

"I wanted to come over," he stammered. His eyes were tearing up. "I wanted to tell you sorry." He wiped his sleeve across his face and paused.

After choking back the tears for a minute, he continued. "I wanted you to know that I am . . ." he stammered. It was hard to understand him through the crying. "That morning he asked me to drive. I didn't want to, but he talked me into it." Derrick couldn't go on he was crying so hard. Robert and I both wrapped our arms around him.

"I'm sorry! I'm sorry I drove. Bobby's a better driver. He would have seen the truck." Derrick's shoulders heaved up and down as he sobbed.

I hadn't realized until now that my own grief had prevented me from seeing anyone else's. My husband's, Matthew's, Derrick's. I knew I needed to look outside myself . . . but how?

* * *

That night, I couldn't sleep, as usual, so I got up and went into the family room. Except for the tiny twinkling lights that reflected in the tree boughs, the room was dark. I was surprised to find Matthew out there as well. He was resting on the sofa.

"How did you get out here?" I asked.

"I walked, Mother," he said smartly. I laughed. He seemed to have more of an attitude since his surgery. Earlier that evening at the family Christmas party, he'd refused to be a shepherd in the Christmas pageant.

"No, don't want to," he declared firmly when I tried to coax him to put on the costume. I tried not to think much of it, considering all he had been through, but something about him seemed different.

I settled into the sofa next to him and stared into the lighted tree.

"I'm goin play bakketball," he said.

"That's sounds fun," I answered.

"That make you happy?"

"If that's what you want to do. Then it will make me happy." I reached over to caress his hand, and he rested his head on my shoulder.

"What's going on here?" my husband whispered from behind, startling Matthew and me. He made his way around the sofa and reached out for Matthew. "Come on, we better get you to bed."

He placed both his hands on Matthew's arms and pulled him up. "Santa Claus can't come if you're out here." He chuckled.

Matthew laughed and threw one arm around his dad. Together they walked back to Matthew's room.

Robert was back in a few minutes with a basketball in his hands, a big bright red bow stuck on the side.

"Where did that come from?" I asked.

"I bought it," he answered and put the ball next to Matthew's stocking. Then he brought the grocery bags of candy, fruit, and nuts from the kitchen. I slid down onto the carpet to help.

"Don't you see what's happening here?" he asked.

"What do you mean?"

"Matthew is trying to replace Bobby."

"What?" I questioned in denial.

"He knows how much you loved watching Bobby play basketball. He thinks if he plays, you'll be happy."

He pushed an orange into the toe of each stocking and followed it with an apple. He then began adding mixed nuts. Meanwhile, I fumbled with the box of candy canes.

"I am happy," I said unconvincingly.

"You can't fool me—or Matthew," he returned.

I didn't respond. I continued running my fingernail under the seam to lift the wrapping. I was getting frustrated; the seam wouldn't budge. Finally, Robert reached over and took the box from me. He pushed his thumb through the cellophane until it tore. He smiled gently and handed me the box.

"I know it's been hard, but you've got to move on. If you can't do it for yourself, do it for Matthew."

I knew he wanted me to be strong. But I wasn't like him. I *wanted* to understand like he did, but it didn't make sense. "I don't understand. I can't understand!" I cried. "Why would God take one life to save another?"

He cleared the grocery bags and slid close to me. I dropped my face onto his shoulder and continued crying.

After some time, he finally said, "That's what the Atonement is."

"What?" I asked, pulling back to get a better look at him.

"The Atonement. God took the life of His Son—His Only Begotten Son. God took His life to save the rest of us."

The words rang true in my head; they penetrated my heart. I gazed down at the candy canes I was holding.

"The shepherd's crook," I said aloud, holding one up. "I've taught my children the meaning of Christmas, but do I really believe it?"

"I think you do," he comforted. "You've just forgotten that you believe."

Had I forgotten?

I watched as he placed the stockings against the rock hearth. I looked around the room until my eyes rested on the tree. As I gazed into the twinkling lights, a peaceful feeling entered my heart. I recognized that feeling.

I'd felt it when I got the phone call about Bobby, I'd felt it in that dark hospital room, and I'd even felt it when we buried our son. I had felt it each time someone offered me words of sympathy or encouragement.

I realized at that moment that the miracle of Christmas is peace—not the peace we think of as the opposite of war but the peace that exists *in* war. The real peace is that even though there is war, even though bad and horrible things happen, even though pain is real and terribly hard to endure, the peace is always there. Because in the very midst of it all, in the most difficult and extreme pain, peace comes from knowing the pain is only temporary.

Because of the Atonement, Bobby will live again. God did give His Son that all of us would live again.

I had been looking at everything in my temporary view, but life isn't temporary. It's eternal. The Atonement is real! I knew it. I felt it.

* * *

Of course, I still missed Bobby, and I still felt the pain and the loss. But after that Christmas Eve, I tried to focus on my faith and feel peace rather than pain.

That's when things began to change—for me and for our family. Matthew got stronger every day. He had energy like we had never seen before. There were times we joked that we wished we could have the old Matthew back. But in truth, we were thrilled to watch him finally be able to thrive.

And he did play basketball, just like he told me. All summer long and into the fall, Matthew trained. He practiced two or three hours a day. He ran mile after mile to get into shape. He lifted weights. He even refused to eat candy or drink soda pop.

"It bad for you," he told us.

That fall, as tryouts approached, I grew more and more concerned. *What if he works this hard and doesn't make the team? How will he deal with the disappointment?* But Robert assured me that it would all work out, and he was right. Matthew made the team.

And though it all seemed too good to be true, game after game, Coach Hughes managed to work Matthew into the rotation. After several games, I told the coach that we didn't expect him to do Matthew any favors.

"Are you kidding?" he said. "Matthew is the one doing me a favor." I assumed he was being nice, so I politely thanked him. Then he looked at me seriously and said, "I mean it. Matthew's attitude is the reason we're undefeated this year. He gives 110 percent all the time, and he demands all the other guys do the same. Do you know what he says before every game? When we're all huddled in the locker room and the guys start getting nervous, Matthew stands up, throws his hands as high as he can, and shouts, 'We're goin win, cause we have bess players!' The guys love him." Then he shook his head. "I don't know what I'll do when he leaves here."

Basketball wasn't the only place Matthew excelled. He had wonderful peer tutors who helped him, and it seemed like every student at the school was his friend.

But even though Matthew was doing well in so many ways, there was one thing that continually troubled me. There were times, randomly, that he wouldn't want to pray, and that just wasn't like him. And recently, his Sunday School teacher told me that he'd asked Matthew to hold up a picture of Jesus, and Matthew had stormed out of the classroom. Though these were small incidents, I was concerned.

-3-

THE DECEMBER MORNING SEEMED COLDER than usual as I heard the phone ring. I glanced toward the clock on the stove—9:15. My heart raced at a fearful pace that I suppose is normal for anyone who has ever received a devastating call. Somehow your heart relives that life-changing moment every time the phone rings. It had been a little more than a year since Bobby's accident. Now, I made my way across the floor and cautiously picked up the phone.

"Mrs. Bailey?" I recognized the voice. It was Mr. Petersen, the principal.

"Yes," I answered, a bit hesitant.

"I've been on the phone with the *Herald*. They have an award, a new one they will be presenting annually to a student in the state who demonstrates certain characteristics. They'd like to name the award for Bobby."

"That's . . . really nice." Tears sprung almost instantly to my eyes at the gesture.

"That's not all," he continued. "This year they would like to present the award to Matthew."

"Wow, really? Oh, Matthew will be thrilled!" I exclaimed.

"Yes, I thought so too." I could hear the smile in his voice as he continued with the details. The award would be presented at the last home basketball game before Christmas break. That was next Friday. He asked me to give Matthew the news and help Matthew prepare a few words to accept the award. I assured him we would work with Matthew, and we both said good-bye.

I was happy for Matthew, but along with the news came a portion of pain. I missed Bobby, and the nearing holiday seemed to intensify my heartache. I was grateful when Matthew came through the door. His sweet innocent nature brought joy and helped me forget the pain.

He was so excited when I told him the news. From then on, he asked me every morning if today was the day he was getting his award. But he refused to let us help him prepare for his acceptance speech.

"I okay," he insisted.

Friday finally arrived. I was a little unsure as to how the presentation would go, but when I asked him if he needed any help, Matthew quickly snapped at me. "I fine. I not a baby." He had definitely become more independent over the past year.

Robert and I made our way to our usual seats just three rows behind the team bench. He was calm, but I kept fidgeting in my seat.

After the national anthem, Mr. Nell from the *Herald* as well as Mr. Petersen walked to the center of the gymnasium. My heart was pounding. Mr. Nell held a large impressive trophy. The base was dark wood, about a foot high. Above the base was a bronze sculpture of several figures: athletes, students, cheerleaders, performing artists—both male and female—forming a human pyramid. The top figure was a graduate with hands stretched up holding firmly to a large, intricately carved heart.

Mr. Petersen held the microphone to Mr. Nell as the editor spoke. "I'm happy to be with you tonight. As many of you know, a year ago, a fine young man from your school lost his life. This young man was a friend to many and an example to all." The audience was quiet.

"And although this young man's life was taken, a part of him lives on. You may not know that this young man was an organ donor and that because of his organs, several lives have been saved." The entire gymnasium erupted with applause.

I wonder if they're grateful, I thought. Those who lived because of Bobby's organs—were they grateful? Matthew was grateful. Matthew was using his heart to do good. What about the others? What were they doing with the new life they had been given? Were they making good use of it?

Instantly, a question came into my mind, *What have you done with the new life He has given you?* I thought of the Atonement. I felt ashamed. He has given me second chances time after time, and I haven't appreciated His sacrifice as I should have. Feeling very humbled, my mind came back to Mr. Nell's voice.

"We do not know the names of all those who received organs from Bobby, but we can tell you about the one who received his heart." Everyone clapped. "Matthew Bailey has earned the attention of people all over this state. He has shown what odds a person can overcome. He, like his brother, has shown us the importance of the human heart." The audience was on their feet.

"The *Herald*, along with many other sponsors, has created an annual award to be given each year to a high school student who has demonstrated qualities of determination and hard work, but also of friendship and encouragement to their schoolmates. The trophy will be showcased at that student's school throughout the year, and the school will receive a monetary donation to use in any way they see fit." The students cheered.

"Now, without dragging this on any further, we would like to present the first annual 'Bobby Bailey: You've Got Heart' award to Matthew Bailey."

Matthew looked around. Everyone in the crowded gymnasium was cheering for him. He walked to Mr. Petersen, who extended his hand for a handshake. But Matthew lifted both arms and hugged the principal. Everyone laughed. He hugged Mr. Nell as well, who was still holding the trophy. The audience laughed again.

Matthew took the trophy with both hands and immediately raised it high above his head, turning to face each section of the audience so they could see it. The crowd cheered and applauded even louder. Mr. Petersen handed the microphone to Mr. Nell and took the trophy from Matthew.

Mr. Nell pulled Matthew to his side and asked, "Matthew, what would you like to say to everyone?"

Matthew leaned over the microphone and said, "Thanku." Everyone laughed.

"Do you know why you have received this award?" Mr. Nell asked.

"I gave my heart to my brother." I squirmed in my seat. People all around the gym were whispering.

Mr. Nell chuckled. "Do you mean your brother gave his heart to you?"

"Yeah. Bobby gave me his heart, so I can play bakketball." The audience cheered, but Matthew continued, "I gave my heart to Bobby so he can meet Jesus." The audience fell silent. I squirmed again. What was Matthew talking about?

Mr. Nell wasn't sure what to do. Finally, he asked, "You gave your heart to Bobby?"

"So he could meet Jesus," Matthew confirmed.

"How did you know Bobby needed your heart?"

"He tode me. He gave me ledder." Matthew unzipped the side pocket of his warm-up jersey and pulled a folded paper from it. He leaned over, whispered something to Mr. Nell, and then spoke into the microphone, "Dad, can you hep me?"

As his dad quickly made his way down onto the floor, Matthew began unfolding the paper. Was that the letter I had read to him the day of Bobby's accident? I had forgotten about it. Now smudged and worn, it had obviously been read many more times.

Matthew hugged his dad and handed him the letter. He leaned into the mic again and said, "My dad's good man." Everyone laughed. Mr. Nell held the microphone for my husband, who gripped the paper with both hands. Matthew clasped his hands behind his back and stood straight like a proud soldier while his dad read the letter.

"To my best brother, Matthew,

"Hey, I've been thinking about Christmas. It's coming up soon. Christmas is the time for miracles, right? We've been praying for a miracle.

"We've all been praying for you to get a new heart, but I just realized that you already have the best heart of anyone I know.

You're nice to everybody, no matter who it is. You're the one always giving, always smiling, and always trying to make everyone else happy.

"*We should be praying for the rest of us to get a new heart. That would be the real miracle. It would be a miracle if the rest of us could trade our hearts in and get new ones just like yours. Isn't that what Jesus wants us to do? Didn't He ask us to change our hearts, to get a new heart? Imagine what a better place the world would be if we all had a heart like yours.*

"*So that's the Christmas miracle I'm praying for. I don't want any presents this year. All I want for Christmas is to change my heart into a heart like yours.*

"*Love, your big brother, Bobby*"

Robert had a hard time fighting the tears as he read. I glanced around the gymnasium. Many people were wiping their eyes. Matthew took the microphone from Mr. Nell then patted his dad on the back.

"My dad's good man." More laughter.

"Thas my ledder from Bobby. He gave to me when I wha sick. Bobby tode me not be scared."

My heart was pounding. I had no idea Matthew had been scared of dying. He'd never told me. I could feel tears spilling onto my cheeks.

"Bobby said if I die Jesus will come to meet me becau I have good heart. He said he wish he had good heart like me." Matthew looked up at everyone and smiled. "So I pray and ask God to give Bobby my heart so Jesus could meet Bobby when he died. And God took out my heart and put it in Bobby."

The place was silent. I looked around. Men, women, even the kids were wiping tears off their cheeks. All eyes were glued on Matthew. For that moment, the gymnasium was filled with complete peace. Even the crowd for the visiting team was in tears. One by one, they began applauding. It was so powerful. It felt like a real miracle. *Miracle?*

We're goin have miraco. I remembered Matthew telling me when I went into his room right after the call about Bobby.

Matthew had been on his knees praying. He must have known. I felt faint.

I began to file through the standing crowd. I saw Matthew raise his arm to wave to everyone. I met up with him and his dad just as the paper's photographer began taking pictures. I wanted to talk to Matthew. I wanted to tell him how proud I was, but he ran off to warm up with his team. It was all so simple to him. Mr. Nell told us the story would be in Sunday's paper.

* * *

"A New Heart for Christmas," it was called. Matthew was so excited to see his picture on the cover of the paper. The article was very nice, and our phone rang all day—neighbors who'd read the story. Even acquaintances from other towns called, saying they'd seen the article. But within a few days, the excitement wore down, and we turned our attention back to getting ready for Christmas.

On the morning of Christmas Eve, I was carrying props for our family Christmas pageant to the garage when something caught my eye. Through the glass of the front door, I saw a glimpse of a figure.

I hadn't heard the doorbell or a knock. I set the props down and headed to the door. "Can I help you?" I called out. The man, already walking away, turned back.

"Ma'am, I'm sorry. I don't mean to bother you," he said, his voice trembling.

It took me only a few seconds to recognize him. He was the driver. The man who hit . . .

I didn't know what to say. I was no longer angry; I could at least show that. "Please, would you like to come in?" I asked.

He walked up the porch steps, and I coaxed him through the door. He kept his head lowered and his eyes fixed on the floor, just as he had in the hospital, but something was different. He had more color in his face. His hair was trimmed.

"I read the story in the paper," he said. "I wanted to come and . . . Well, I've come by before, but I just couldn't—" He stopped. He trembled, and his fingers caressed his hat. He couldn't look at me. I stretched my hand out and placed it on his.

"It's okay," I said. "Our family is okay."

"Thank you, Mrs. Bailey," he said, his voice cracking as he choked back the tears. "Your family, you changed my life."

"What?" I asked.

"Your husband. He was so kind, so forgiving." He lifted his head a little, enough for me to see his eyes. They were bright, not hollow as before. He gazed down again. "I, uh, prayed," he stammered. "It had been a long time, you know. But I did. I prayed, and then I wanted to call my son. My son and I . . . well, years ago . . . We hadn't spoken." He broke into tears. "I, uh, well, I finally . . . called him and . . . and he wanted to talk to me! We talked. Well, I have my family back, and I wanted to thank you but . . . how could I when I, well, you know . . . caused you so much pain?"

I raised both my arms and put them around him. "We're fine. Everything is okay." He pulled himself from my embrace; it was obvious the close contact was uncomfortable to him.

"I didn't want to bother you. I'm on a run"—he pointed through the glass door to his truck—"just passing through. I just wanted you to know . . . because, well, when I read the story about your boys, you know . . ." His tall thin shoulders hunched over.

"Then it was all worth it," I said, feeling a new strength build up inside of me. He looked up at me. This was the first that he'd allowed his eyes to meet mine.

"What do you mean?" he asked.

"If it brought you to God, it makes the sacrifice, the pain—everything—it makes it all worth it."

He nodded. "Thank you, Mrs. Bailey," he said humbly and reached for the door.

"Will you be home for Christmas?" I asked.

"Yes, I'll get home tomorrow morning."

"Can I get you something for the road?" I asked, headed to the kitchen.

"Oh no! I'm fine," he called out, but I was already scurrying around, pulling a package together.

"Don't leave," I hollered. "It'll take me just a minute." Luckily, I had purchased extra baskets, and it was easy to find a surplus of food and goodies to fill one.

"Here, this should make the trip feel a little more festive," I told him and held up the basket. He graciously accepted, thanked me, and pulled the door open.

"Merry Christmas!" I blurted out and lunged forward to hug him. He allowed me this time. Even pressed one arm around me.

"Merry Christmas," he replied. He walked out and began down the sidewalk.

"Stop by, will you? Whenever you pass through?" I called out.

He didn't say anything but nodded as he climbed up into the cab. The engine rumbled as he pulled away from the curb. He turned and waved at me.

The pain was gone. I hugged the stranger who had killed my son and I felt like I was hugging a friend. I was healed.

Was this what forgiveness felt like? Was this why Robert had healed so fast? Was it because he was able to forgive so quickly? I had no idea that forgiveness could be so powerful. But it was true. I was healed. Another miracle!

I was still in such a trance when the phone rang that I didn't even feel the pain once connected to a ringing telephone. I didn't feel fear or pain; I only heard a phone ringing.

"Hello."

"Mrs. Bailey, this is Mr. Nell from the *Herald*. Sorry to bother you on Christmas Eve, but I thought you might want to hear the news."

"What news?" I asked, a bit curious.

"A New Heart for Christmas," he exclaimed. "The story about Bobby and Matthew. You can't imagine the response. We've had phone calls, letters. People have been touched by the story. They're being kinder to their neighbors. They're doing more for their families, coworkers, and friends. Hearts are changing.

Hearts are being healed because of your boys. I wanted you to know."

"Thank you," I answered.

"It's a real Christmas miracle!" he exclaimed.

"Yes, I guess it is," I answered. "Merry Christmas."

"Merry Christmas to you," he replied.

Another miracle, I thought as I hung up the phone. We'd had a lot of those lately. I thought back to that morning again, when Matthew told me, "We're goin have miraco!"

I thought of him kneeling, leaned against the bed, praying for God to give Bobby his heart. My mind began putting it together.

Suddenly it all made sense. That's why sometimes he wouldn't want to pray. And why he didn't want to hold the picture of Jesus. And why he didn't want to be a shepherd in the family Christmas pageant last year.

Matthew had always loved being in the Christmas pageant. He was six the first year he'd had enough strength to participate. He'd been so excited! He stood still as I draped the towels over his shoulders and his head. He was brave when it was time to go on stage, and he was quiet during everyone's speaking parts. He did his part just like he was taught and even scooted back with the other shepherds so the wise men could present their gifts to the Christ child. But Matthew surprised all of us when we were about to sing the final carol and he stepped forward and asked Mary, "Can I hode him?" It was so precious. He'd melted our hearts, and we did the pageant that way every year since.

I hadn't been overly concerned when he'd refused to participate last year, knowing he was recovering from heart surgery, but now it was clear there had been a much bigger reason.

Robert was downstairs wrapping gifts. *He'll know what to do*, I thought and ran down to talk to him.

"I know what's bothering Matthew," I said, startling him a bit. We had talked often about our concerns of his behavior.

"I'm listening," he responded.

"I think Matthew believes that he won't meet Jesus when he dies."

"What?" he asked.

"He thinks that God gave his heart to Bobby, so now he doesn't have a good heart anymore."

"Of course!" he exclaimed. "I think you're right. Don't worry about it. I'll talk to him."

I knew my husband could find a way to help Matthew understand. He was good at that. I hurried to load the props into the car and gathered the articles for Matthew's costume.

After loading the food and gifts into the backseat, the three of us buckled up and were on our way. The family party would be at my brother Dave's house this year. That was well over an hour's drive. We spent the first part of the drive talking about the truck driver and the call from Mr. Nell at the paper. Matthew was excited to have all this news about him. He reminded us a few times that he brought the paper to show everyone in the family.

Finally, my husband changed the conversation. "Matthew, guess what I learned today."

"Wha, Dad?" he asked eagerly.

"I found out that if someone gives away their heart, they will get to see Jesus when they die."

"Tha not true, Dad. You just sain that."

"No, it's true. I looked it up because I was thinking about how you gave away your good heart."

"Really, Dad. Tha true?" he asked. I had been right. He really thought that he couldn't meet Jesus because he'd given away his heart.

My husband continued. "Do you know what Jesus said?"

"No," Matthew answered.

"In the Bible, Jesus said a good man out of good treasure of his heart bringeth forth that which is good."

"What tha mean, Dad?" Matthew asked.

"It means that when you give away something good, you bring back something good. Because you gave away your good heart, God brought a good heart back to you. God gave you Bobby's heart. And you made it a very special and good heart."

"Will Jesus meet me when I die?" Matthew asked.

"Jesus will be so happy to meet you when you die," his dad encouraged him. "But we hope that won't be for a very long time." We all laughed together. I leaned back in my seat.

Another miracle, I thought, and I tried to count in my head how many I had witnessed this Christmas season—there had been a lot.

Matthew played the part of a shepherd in the family Christmas pageant just as he had in years past. And just after the wise men presented their gifts, he stepped forward and asked Mary, "Can I hode him?"

And as Matthew cradled the baby in his arms, we all sang out together, "Joy to the world, the Lord is come, Let earth receive her king!"

I truly felt it. I felt the joy of Christmas like I had never felt before. I understood more than ever how important the gift of His Son was to us.

But it was the next line that really got to me. "Let every heart prepare Him room." My sons taught me about this. I couldn't help but remember Bobby's letter to Matthew.

So that's the Christmas miracle I'm praying for. I don't want any presents this year. All I want for Christmas is to change my heart into a heart like yours.

Although it took the miracle of surgery to give Matthew a new heart, one that would get him through this life, Bobby had learned of the greatest miracle of all. He learned that a person could receive a new heart without surgery. Bobby knew that to receive this new heart, he needed to make room—to make room for Christ, make room for family, make room for those in need, and make room for everyone he met.

It was easy for Matthew to make room in his heart, as it is for many special needs children. For the rest of us, it takes a little more effort. We're more distracted, I suppose, but it is possible.

Let *every* heart prepare Him room.

Christmas means different things to different people, but for me, it now means finding room in my heart, maybe even finding a new heart. But that is the miracle! I've witnessed a lot of miracles, but the greatest of all is that we can change. Because of Him, we can change our old heart. We can have, each of us . . .

A new heart for Christmas.

About the Author

DEBBIE HARMAN ATTENDED SNOW COLLEGE, where met she met her husband. They live in a 120-year-old home in Manti, Utah. Debbie and her husband have four children, seven grandsons, and one granddaughter. Debbie has served in all ward auxiliaries and as a stake Young Women president and Snow College Stake Relief Society president. She currently serves as the Laurel adviser in her ward.